MOTHER GOOSE

Sticker Fun Word Book

Illustrated by Carolynn Geer

DERRYDALE BOOKS
New York • Avenel

HOW TO USE YOUR
MOTHER GOOSE STICKER FUN BOOK

In each rhyme, some words have been left out. Find the correct stickers for those words from the sticker pages at the back of the book. Place the stickers in the correct spaces. The stickers are grouped by pages to help you. If you would like a hint, the missing words are listed in a special box for each rhyme.

Created and manufactured by arrangement with
Ottenheimer Publishers, Inc.
© 1993 Ottenheimer Publishers, Inc.
All rights reserved. SF-818D
This 1995 edition published by DERRYDALE BOOKS,
distributed by Random House Value Publishing,
40 Engelhard Avenue, Avenel, New Jersey 07001.
Printed in Hong Kong.

ISBN: 0-517-10309-5

8 7 6 5 4 3 2

TABLE OF CONTENTS

Hey Diddle, Diddle

Hey diddle, diddle,

The ____ and the ____ ,

The cow jumped over the ____ ;

The little ____ laughed

To see such sport,

And the ____ ran away with the ____ .

My Sticker Words
cat
fiddle
moon
dog
dish
spoon

Hickety, Pickety, My Black Hen

Hickety, pickety, my black hen,

She lays  for gentlemen;

come every day

To see what my black hen doth lay;

Sometimes nine and sometimes ten,

Hickety, pickety, my black   .

My Sticker Words
eggs
Gentlemen
hen

6

Hickory, Dickory, Dock

Hickory, dickory, dock,

The mouse ran up the clock.

The   struck one,

The   ran down,

Hickory, dickory, dock!

My Sticker Words
clock
mouse

Humpty Dumpty

Humpty Dumpty sat on a  ;

had a great fall.

All the king's

And all the king's

Couldn't put Humpty Dumpty

Together again.

My Sticker Words
wall
Humpty Dumpty
horses
men

11

I Saw a Ship A-Sailing

I saw a  a-sailing,

A-sailing on the _____,

And, oh, but it was laden

With pretty things for thee.

There were biscuits in the cabin

And _____ in the hold;

The sails were made of silk,

And the masts were all of gold.

My Sticker Words

ship	mice
sea	chains
apples	duck

The four-and-twenty sailors

That stood between the decks

Were four-and-twenty white

With  about their necks.

The captain was a

With a packet on his back,

And when the ship began to move

The captain said, "Quack! Quack!"

Jack and Jill

Jack and Jill went up the hill

To fetch a [pail] of water.

Jack fell down and broke his crown

And [Jill] came tumbling after.

Then up Jack got and home did trot

As fast as he could caper.

He went to [bed] and wrapped his head

In [vinegar] and brown paper.

My Sticker Words

pail	bed
Jill	vinegar

Little Boy Blue

Little Boy Blue, come blow your ___ ,

The sheep is in the meadow,

The ___ is in the ___ .

Where is the ___ who looks after the ___ ?

He's under the ___ , fast asleep!

My Sticker Words

horn	boy
cow	sheep
corn	haystack

Mary Had a Little Lamb

Mary had a little lamb,

Its fleece was white as   ;

And everywhere that Mary went

The   was sure to go.

It followed her to school one day,

Which was against the rule;

It made the   laugh and play

To see a lamb at   .

My Sticker Words
snow   children
lamb   school

Mary, Mary, Quite Contrary

Mary, Mary, quite contrary,

How does your garden grow?

With silver  and cockle 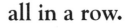,

And pretty all in a row.

My Sticker Words
bells

shells

maids

My Sticker Words

buckle   sticks
shoe   hen
door   plate

One, Two, Buckle My Shoe

One, two, [ ] my [ ] ,

Three, four, shut the [ ] ,

Five, six, pick up [ ] ,

Seven, eight, lay them straight,

Nine, ten, a big fat [ ] ;

Eleven, twelve, dig and delve,

Thirteen, fourteen, maids are courting,

Fifteen, sixteen, maids in the kitchen,

Seventeen, eighteen, maids are waiting,

Nineteen, twenty, my [ ] is empty!

Old King Cole

Old Cole

Was a merry old soul,

And a merry old soul was he.

He called for his   ,

And he called for his   ,

And he called for his   three.

My Sticker Words
King
pipe
bowl
fiddlers

Old Mother Hubbard

Old Mother Hubbard

Went to the cupboard

To get her poor dog a 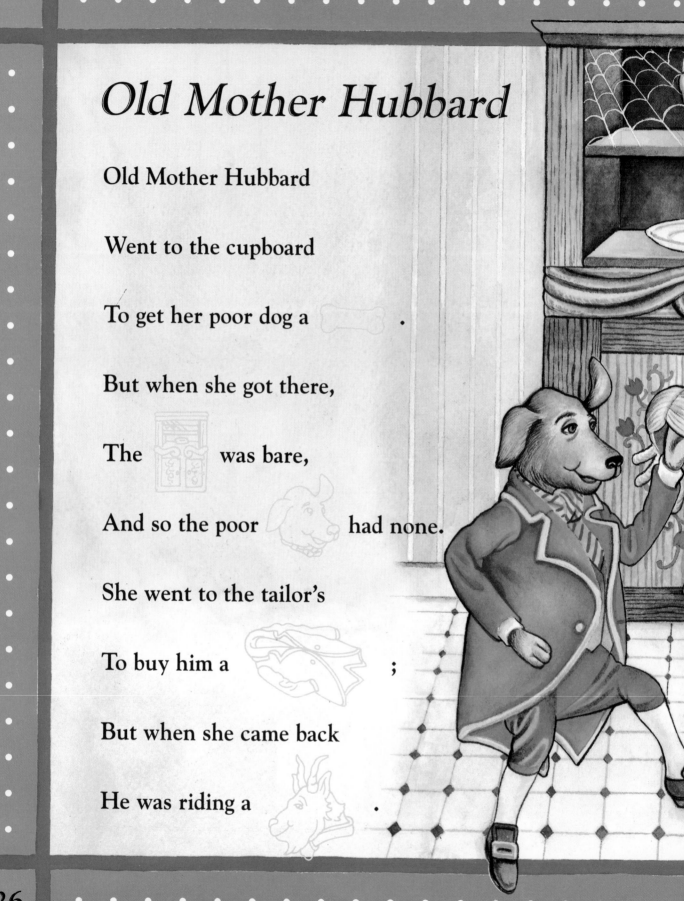 .

But when she got there,

The ▭ was bare,

And so the poor 🐕 had none.

She went to the tailor's

To buy him a 🎩 ;

But when she came back

He was riding a 🐐 .

She went to the barber's

To buy him a  ;

But when she came back

He was dancing a jig.

She went to the cobbler's

To buy him some ;

But when she came back

He was reading the !

My Sticker Words

bone	goat
cupboard	wig
dog	shoes
coat	news

Pussy Cat, Pussy Cat, Where Have You Been?

Pussy cat, pussy [cat], where have you been?

I've been to London to visit the [queen].

Pussy cat, pussy cat, what did you do there?

I frightened a little [mouse] under her [chair].

My Sticker Words

cat

queen

mouse

chair

The Lion and the Unicorn

The lion and the unicorn

Fighting for the   ,

The lion chased the

All about the town.

Some gave them white   ,

And some gave them brown;

Some gave them plum

And chased them out of   !

My Sticker Words
crown   bread
unicorn   cake
town

31

Sing a Song of Sixpence

Sing a song of  ,

A pocket full of rye,

Four and twenty

Baked in a pie.

When the was opened,

The birds began to sing.

Now wasn't that a dainty

To set before the ?

My Sticker Words

sixpence   pie
blackbirds   dish
king

This Little Pig

This little pig went to market,

This little pig stayed home,

This little pig had some ⬭ ,

This little 🐷 had none,

And this little pig cried, "Wee, wee, wee!"

All the way home!

My Sticker Words
roast beef
pig

Twinkle, Twinkle, Little Star

Twinkle, twinkle, little ⭐ .

How I wonder what you are!

Up above the 🌍 so high,

Like a 💎 in the sky.

In the dark blue sky you keep,

And often through my 🪟 peep,

For you never shut your 👁 ,

Till the ☀ is in the sky.

My Sticker Words

star	curtains
world	eye
diamond	sun

Wee Willie Winkie

Wee Willie Winkie runs through the town,

Upstairs and downstairs in his   ,

Rapping at the   , crying through the   ,

Are the children all in   ?

For now it's eight o'clock!

My Sticker Words
nightgown
window
lock
bed

39

As I Was Going to St. Ives

As I was going to St. Ives,

I met a  with seven wives.

Each (wife) had seven sacks,

Each (sack) had seven cats,

Each (cat) had seven kittens.

(Kittens), cats, sacks, and wives,

How many were going to St. Ives?

My Sticker Words

man

wife

sack

cat

kittens

Baa, Baa, Black Sheep

Baa, baa, black 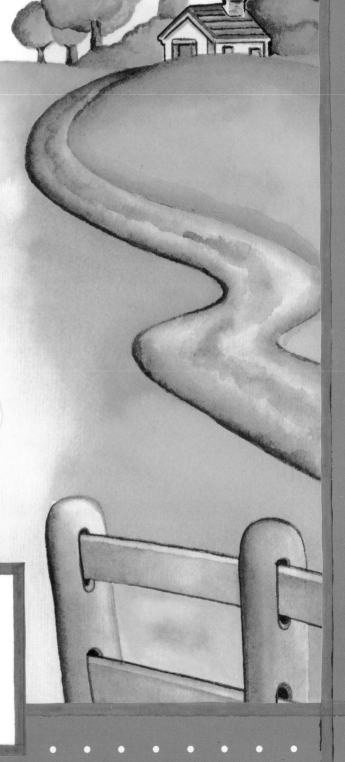 ,

Have you any wool?

Yes, sir, yes, sir,

Three   full:

One for the master,

And one for the dame,

And one for the little

Who lives down the lane.

My Sticker Words
sheep
bags
boy

Ride a Cock Horse to Banbury Cross

Ride a cock horse to Banbury Cross

To see a fine  upon a white

With ⟡⟡ on her fingers

And ⊙⊙ on her toes,

She shall have music wherever she goes!

My Sticker Words
lady
horse
rings
bells

A Cat Came Fiddling

A cat came fiddling out of a

With a pair of   under her arm.

She could sing nothing but "Fiddle cum fee,

The   has married the honey   ."

Pipe, cat! Dance, mouse!

We'll have a wedding at our good   .

My Sticker Words
barn
bagpipes
mouse
bee
house

Little Jack Horner

Little Jack Horner

Sat in a corner,

Eating a Christmas 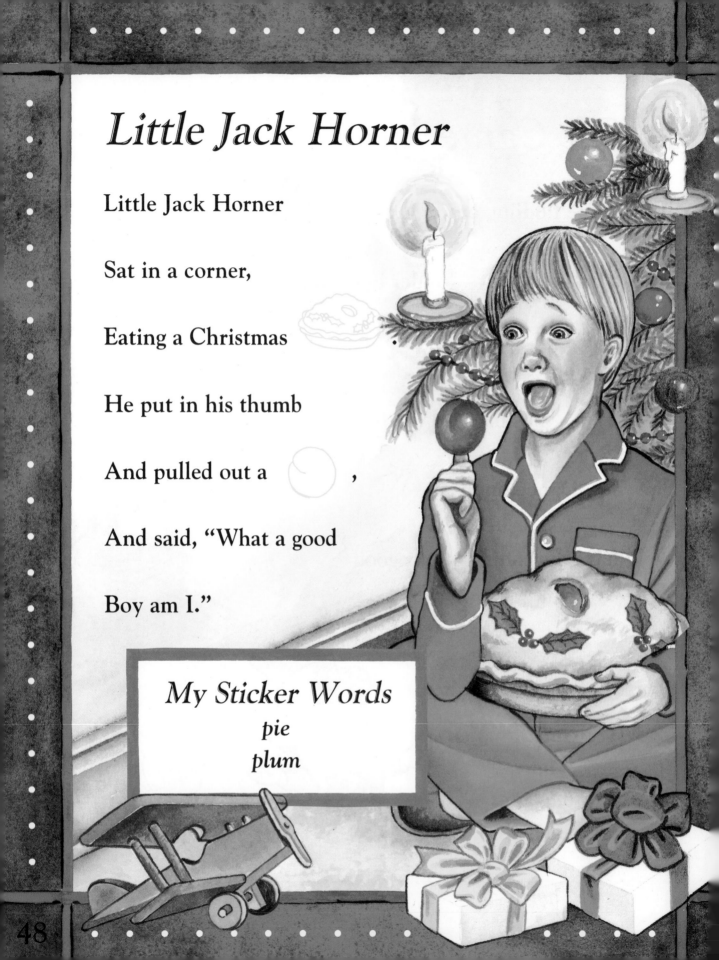.

He put in his thumb

And pulled out a   ,

And said, "What a good

Boy am I."

My Sticker Words
pie
plum

48

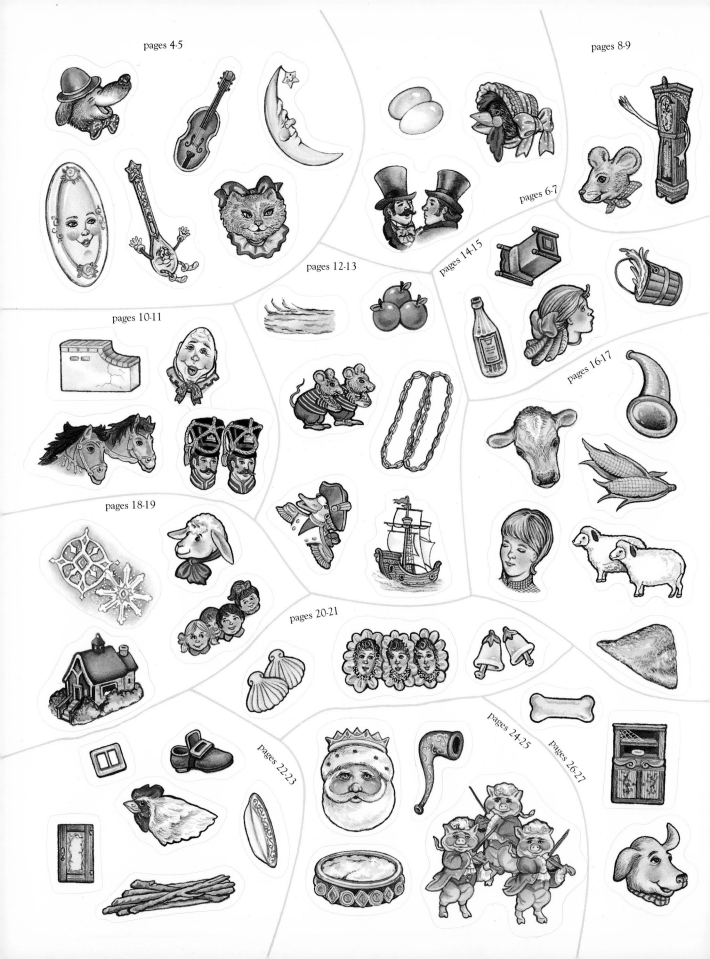

pages 4-5

pages 8-9

pages 6-7

pages 12-13

pages 14-15

pages 10-11

pages 16-17

pages 18-19

pages 20-21

pages 22-23

pages 24-25

pages 26-27